Feel

Heal

Love

REFLECTIONS ON FINDING
YOUR TRUE SELF THROUGH LOSS

DILINE ABUSHABAN

ISBN: 978-1-913-47892-6

Dedicated to

Mama - who I was humbled to learn that the content of the book helped her to find peace in her past losses

Baba - the wise one

And to all the refugee families I worked with in the past few years, who despite their deep losses often showed courage and everlasting resilience

Table of Contents

Introduction...1

First steps in dealing with your pain 3

Realise it. Accept it..5

Release it. Feel it fully..7

Patience 9

Orchids...11

Avoid victimising yourself 12

Reflect..14

Change the way you look at it...............................15

A call to change 18

Things you will learn through the journey..............21

Meanings and messages all around you 23

People change...26

About expectations...29

You will learn to disconnect 30

Never give up on yourself 31

Forgiveness..33

Give unconditionally..34

Decisions 37

Keeping busy 39

Just start 41

You will know no worries 43

Detach yourself from people and worldly things .. 44

You will be free 46

Silence 48

The power of words 50

Purification 53

You realise your true age 56

Home will also have a different meaning 58

Things to help you in the healing journey 59

Walking 61

Talking 63

Good friendships 64

Writing 65

Art 66

Fasting 69

Breathe 70

Heal through nature 71

Contemplate 72

Trees...76

Waterfalls 78

Mountains 80

Seeds.. 82

Listen.. 83

Touch.. 84

Smell... 86

Look and see 88

An innocent smile... 89

Pray...90

The outcome 91

Celebrating the re-birth of your authentic self....... 93

Your face will change – a lot 94

You will be content....................................... 95

Love is the secret of life................................97

Love 98

Introduction

This is a book for you, yes, you my fellow human. I appreciate that you decided to read it, because it was written for you and gifted to you.

This book might be small, but its meaning is deep. You can only understand it if you read it with your full heart, because it was written with my full heart to yours. Make this book your friend that you need when you can't find someone who understands your pain.

This book was written amid mountains, between valleys, in the heart of forests, on the shores of rivers and seas. There were many witnesses to the writing of this book, including bugs, bees, wasps, snails, birds and many trees. They all had something to whisper to the pages of the book. So be aware of that. All those creatures are part of you and were sending you messages of love to help you through your loss, calling you to reconnect with them, with your mother nature.

This book is for those who experienced loss which I believe is part of the human experience. When I say loss, I don't merely mean the loss of a loved one. It can be losing a dear thing in your life whether it's a home, wealth or your health. It can also be betrayals or even moments of loss and uncertainty, when you lose a sense of who you really are.

The reflections and lessons in this book are an outcome of my experiences of loss, which I know at the time, broke my heart, but as the time passed I became more and more grateful for those experiences, as they actually opened my heart to regain wisdom, truth and light.

I believe that each one of you have this too. That is the reason I wrote this book, to help awaken all this within you.

To help you find the gains in your losses. To help you be brave to be fully, proudly and never apologetically YOU. To help you understand that all that you have been, or are going through is not a loss, but indeed, is the path that was made for you to regain your soul and get it back on track. To help you win yourself, and if you win yourself, you never really lost anything.

First steps in dealing with your pain

Realise it. Accept it

One of the most common mistakes we make when dealing with loss, is falling into a state of denial. Or saying to yourself: I have got this. OK, even if you have, that is great. But you need to realise that it happened, something that you did not want to happen whatever it was; a loss of a loved one, loss of trust, loss of health or wealth whatever kind of 'loss' you went through, realise it. Realise it was not an easy thing to go through. It is difficult and you acknowledge this fully. Have no resistance to it at all, feel the pain. Realise that your heart broke because of this loss and that you have the right to feel deep pain.

Grieve as much as you need to, but never fall into the trap of denial.

The best part of realising it is to realise that it all happened for you, not against you and this realisation is the game changer! This will help you accept it; acceptance will help you heal in the best possible way. Yes, it is not easy to lose someone or something precious to us; it is not easy to accept it but you can train yourself. Acceptance will help in putting the pieces of your heart back together again.

Release it. Feel it fully

Let it all out.

Empty yourself.

Grieve as much as you need and as long as you need.

Write it all out.

Wash it out.

Wash it with tears.

Tears have the power to stop the fire inside you, then wash out the ashes that the fire has left.

Tears will help you move away from rejecting or resisting the loss.

Tears will help you feel the pain fully. They will empower you to move out of the pain and move on with your life as they allowed you to let it all out.

When you cry.

The pain can fly.

Your heart will be washed before your eyes.

And the joy will be unlocked and ready to meet you nearby.

Crying is the language of purifying your soul

and bringing life back to it.

So, cry.

Cry whenever things get overwhelming.

Cry when you cannot explain why.

Cry for the sake of crying.

Cry to express your humanity.

Cry to take all the weight off your chest.

Cry so your soul can fly.

Fly up high.

Patience

Patience, oh how significant this is throughout your journey! The real and most significant patience is at the start of your shock. The way that you decide to react, decides the direction you will have to take: suffering or growth. If you decide to react with patience from the beginning, it will pave a journey of growth for you.

Patience will help you keep yourself together. It will help you face what you are going through with a sense of acceptance, without resistance or denial.

Patience is the key to fulfilment. It springs from strength and needs to be cultivated over time, as it takes effort and courage to control yourself – to be a truly patient person.

As you will learn patience through loss, it will be easy for you to have patience in the daily life experiences.

Patience is to smile although you have so many reasons to have grumpy face.

Patience is to answer a bad message in a peaceful manner.

Patience is to keep going when all the reasons and circumstances are pushing you to give up.

Patience is to keep positive no matter how negative things can seem.

Patience is waiting for something to happen with a content heart.

Patience is waiting with strong faith, believing that what you are waiting for will happen, no matter how impossible it may seem.

Patience is to never complain.

Patience does not know blame.

Patience is never feeling like a victim.

Patience is the main key to success, contentment and to living a fulfilling life.

Orchids

They are great at teaching patience. They go on a long sleep; you think they will never bloom. They need care, attention and most importantly: faith.

After a good wait, they will give you delightful flowers, which will last for a long time. Orchids teach you a lesson: if you wait with patience, you deserve a beautiful gift after.

Avoid victimising yourself

Believe from the very beginning of any loss or hardship that it is here to serve you and not to serve against you. This will mean that you are not a victim. You are not meant to be one, even if everyone in the world thinks you are.

Never think that of yourself, for a number of reasons. Feeling or thinking with a victim mentality will only provide you with weakness, sadness and negative vibrations. A victim mentality will only fuel negative emotions like anger and revenge or blame. Blame means that you are not taking responsibility for what you are going through; instead, you are blaming someone else.

When you do not come from a position of responsibility, you will disempower yourself with your own actions; you will force feelings of weakness and helplessness on yourself and instead of investing your time finding solutions and good ways of dealing with your issues, you will waste your time blaming others or thinking of revenge.

All this will steal your peace; it will defeat the purpose of your loss. Instead of taking it as an opportunity to purify your heart, you will add more filth to it!

So please, take responsibility, which does not mean blaming yourself, of course not. It means that you are taking responsibility for how to deal with it in the best way. This will give you all the power in the world, as taking responsibility means you are coming from a position of power and authority rather than weakness and helplessness.

Reflect

The main and most effective way to change your mindset about your situation, whether it is a trauma or any life tribulation, is to reflect.

You can ask yourself:

What is the real message behind what happened? Did I play a role in it? How can this be in my favour?

Reflecting empowers you to take responsibility for what you went through or are going through; it liberates you from guilt, blame, anger or hatred.

When you take responsibility, you will have the power to change your situation, control yourself, your thoughts and your emotions. When you have control over this, all aspects of your life will change and everything in the whole world will change to serve you, even your trauma; it was there for you, not against you.

Change the way you look at it

Reflecting will help you change the way you look at your loss. You and only you have the power to see it as a gift, or go the other way and see it as a misery; it is totally your choice.

One of the biggest limitations that human beings often have is being single-minded about judging things and events from the outside. Being too fixated about what good is and what bad is. We think of many things, events, lifestyles as being 'good' for us. We are being passed those assumptions and ideas from family, the media, our networks or the society we live in.

Sometimes, we can really like something and see it as a good thing when in reality, it is not. We keep asking for it, wishing for it to happen to us, thinking it will fulfil our greatest happiness, then when it happens, we finally realise that it was not a 'good' thing and wish that we never hoped for it to happen. So, instead of learning this the hard way, we can try and learn it from today.

Ask yourself whenever something 'bad' happens: what's the good in this? Loss is one of those things that is often perceived as 'bad' but if you can dig deep, you can always find 'good' in it. Of course, this does not mean forgetting to grieve as mentioned before. For example, if you view it as an opportunity for connecting with yourself, something that you never cared about before this loss, the pages of the book will take you through how this is possible.

Also, when you have been wishing for something to happen for so long but it doesn't, ask: what could be bad about what I'm wishing for? Maybe there's a good reason it's not happening. For example, that trip that you really wanted to take part in despite the signs of delay, missed buses and more, you still insisted to go because you viewed it as not just 'good' but extraordinary. Remember how you ended up with a sprained ankle and weren't able to walk properly for weeks! The 'good' that you insisted getting ended up with ruining the blessing of walking for weeks. This can apply to anything, like a job that you really wanted or a course that you thought fits you well but you didn't get a place, try to look beyond the disap-pointment. It could be a shortcut for you, instead of starting a path that you wouldn't have enjoyed and stopped after realising that.

When you practice this way of thinking, you will always find contentment in every situation.

A call to change

Losses and life's tribulations can always be a call for a change; most people ignore the call and get too busy and distracted with feelings of shame, victimising, guilt or blame.

Yes, change can be uncomfortable; it can be very difficult. Yes, it will be full of bumps, holes and barriers, but it will all be worth it at the end. It is inevitable for your growth.

Change to grow. The uncomfortable feeling will surely fade away and will be replaced with joy, peace and many good things will come your way.

It will be full of sacrifice.

You will pay a price, the financial price will be the 'cheapest' one! You will pay in energy, breaths, tears and fears. You will face critiques, unfair judgements and untruthful stories. You will fight many battles by yourself; you will have to stand up for yourself.

You will no longer be that quiet, too nice person that you wanted to keep, but you will bring the best out of you. You will still be able to deal with things nicely and as peacefully as you can. You will need to give up some thoughts and habits that had never served you any good and replace them with good ones.

You will need to read, read and read!

You will invest in yourself. You will give up relying too much on people, as you will know that no one will be able to carry your 'pain' for you; no one will understand what you are going through. No one will be able to truly support you as much as you can support yourself.

Things you will

learn through

the journey

Meanings and messages all around you

There is a meaning in everything, in every person, event or situation that comes across your path. Every situation that did not go as you wished for had a message that it wanted you to understand. That bus that you could not catch – you might have distracted yourself by shouting at the driver instead of thinking about the message/meaning behind it. Organise your time better next time. Or the meaning could be that we hunt for many things in our lives but do not manage to catch them because of the lack of organisation, planning or action-taking. That bus wanted to bring this to your attention.

That time when your card was rejected when you went to pay, you may have cried or complained about your situation at the time. However, the message was that it was time to find a new job, improve yourself and your career. Look within you for where you can give more, so you gain more and become more abundant.

That relationship which ended did not happen to break your heart, no, that was not the message. It happened to help you grow, find a new path and search for fulfilment within yourself instead of looking for it in the eyes of others.

That person, who you moaned about on the street or on a train, came to make you notice that you have that exact issue that caused your dislike of them, to help you purify that issue from your system and become a better person. For example, you see someone crossing the road without looking out for traffic, waiting for the drivers to stop if they see them, and not valuing their own life and leaving it to others to avoid hitting them. Maybe you will judge them for that, but if you dig deep, they came to make you aware that you do the same thing when you seek the value of your life from others rather than yourself. Maybe not in the same way as our friends who cross the road, but by fearing people's judgements or constantly seeking approval from them. Your friend who crossed the road came to purify you from this, only if you reflect and pay attention.

Little everyday events that we hardly reflect on, try to push us towards the role we have to achieve for humankind, we need to make sure to read the signs and reflect on the meanings and messages of every situation to fully achieve our role for humanity.

Because each and every one of us has a very specific role in this life. Events, things and people who come to our journey push us towards this role.

When we turn a blind eye to all this and do not reflect often, it's like we refuse to do our mission in this world, which means that we will be a cause of the dysfunction that is happening.

Pay attention, become more aware and do not ignore the signs. If you do, things will take longer to be fulfilled in your life and you will miss out on many opportunities to grow.

People change

Before going through your 'loss', during the journey, you may have tried hard to please people. You may have put too much out of your soul to gain their 'approval'. You may have become apologetic for things that you never did or never thought could cause disturbance to anyone. You may have said many 'yeses' when your soul was saying 'no'. Your loss made you realise that this was all pointless. It had only eaten you up and drained your precious energy.

You learned that people change – many will never be pleased. Many will forget all your goodness for a tiny flaw. Because they see through the eye of their hearts. That, my friend, you have no control over. That also means that no matter what you do, say or invest you can never win. You will never look good in the eyes of the ones who are troubled within. That loss came to drive your focus in the right direction. Towards you and towards the beauty of the universe around you. When you start doing this, everything else will also turn towards you. Everything else will work in your favour. You did not come to this earth to worry about pleasing others. It is your journey; it is your path, so walk it arming yourself with love and compassion.

Those who matter, those who share your passions, those who share your purpose will join you on the path, without you making any effort, without you making any sacrifice, without you putting any burden on your soul. When those join the path, they will help you to connect more with your soul; they will also help you to keep connected with your purpose. They will encourage you to rise and strive. You will all help each other to reach the destination that you were made for. Each person you meet has a purpose in your life that contributes to your growth. Some will teach you a lesson; others will make you aware of some attributes that you need to avoid. Some can inspire you.

If you are lucky enough a few will help you see the spark in you, those are the best ones you can ever meet. They challenge you to pull yourself out of your comfort zone and to come out of your shell. Even if you have not met any of those, yet, please make sure to be this person in someone else's journey.

Your loss will teach you that the significance of people is not counted by the time you spent with them or the closeness of your relationship, but rather by the way they made you feel about yourself, the effect they left on your heart and the breeze they left on your soul.

You can spend a lifetime with someone and all they left was bruises on your heart.

Remember: those who were not with you in the middle of the storm, should never be back in your life when you arrive safely to the shore.

All your experiences with people will make you self-reliant, you will learn that you are enough if you have faith in yourself.

About expectations

You will expect so much from yourself. Expect many blessings, abilities and achievements. Expect with no limits.

When speaking about expectations from others, however, this needs to be limited. When you expect too much, you give the green light for disappointment in your life. Expect good from people but not too much. Expecting too much from people, can also lead you to fall into the trap of blaming and anger. In both cases this will affect your mental and emotional wellbeing.

You can easily avoid all this by limiting your expectations of people, and know deeply and with pure love that each one of them is going through their own journey too. If they did not meet the 'limited' expectations, it is because they are also humans and are limited too.

You will learn to disconnect

You will learn the value of your own time. Away from everyone and everything. Only you and your maker. This is the most precious time that you can have in your day, week or month.

You will learn that you need to disconnect from all the platforms and devices that were made to keep you connected with everyone apart from yourself. They were made to distract you from the most important connection of all: the connection with your soul.

Imagine yourself as a device and your soul is the WIFI, you need this connection to find the right answers for you, to find your truth. Your loss will make you aware of this. You will learn to disconnect from everything to reconnect with yourself. You will build your own cave and visit it whenever you need to check up on yourself, how you are getting on and where you are standing in relation to the purpose that you were made for.

Never give up on yourself

You will learn to never give up on yourself. No matter how hard it gets, chin up. The most dangerous trap to fall into is to give up on yourself.

Yes, you lost someone or something that was dear to you. Yes; it is a very difficult thing to go through. Yes, your heart broke. But do not let this make you lose yourself.

Always keep your faith in yourself and know that you would not have gone through this trial if you were not capable of handling it; you have the wisdom and compassion to be able to put yourself back together again. You are able to pull yourself out of this with your thoughts, attitudes and actions that follow on this principle.

This will make you learn a lot about yourself and reconnect with things and skills that you had within you but never realised or acknowledged. Or maybe you did but you ignored them; now is the time for all the hobbies, talents and skills to come out. You will learn how beautiful you are. You will learn to befriend yourself, to love yourself.

The most precious gift that your trauma can give you is that it enables you to see the beauty of your being, to cherish yourself, which you will know comes from a higher source that made you with perfection.

The biggest achievement is to enjoy your own company.

How amazing it is when you hear yourself saying: 'I am glad to be you, it is so easy to live with you without dramas or complexities. You are so simple, and simplicity is the key to tranquillity.'

I remember being very impressed by the positive attitude of a girl who had lost her father. I mentioned this to her mum and she replied that she taught her daughter that 'you are enough, people come and go, so be happy with yourself.' What a powerful lesson to teach her daughter to cope with the loss of her father!

Forgiveness

You need to forgive to be able to fully let go of your past. You will forgive the events, people and most importantly, you will forgive yourself. You forgive because you deserve the peace that springs from forgiveness.

Be assured that justice will be achieved, whether you forgive or not. Choose peace over battle. Let go of them and forgive them. Forgiveness is one form of freedom.

You free yourself from the past, from anger and regrets. You deserve to be free!

Give unconditionally

Giving has a mysteriously satisfying power. When you give, you actually give to yourself before giving anyone else.

Never think that giving will make you have less. Actually, the more you give, the more you have and the more you get. Imagine if we all practice this, no one will ever be in need and abundance will spread all over the world.

One of the worst attributes of human beings is being obsessed with money. This makes many very protective of their wealth; avoiding giving for fear of decrease, not realising that in reality this exact thought is what takes abundance away from them. Even if they had billions in their bank accounts, they will never have enough and they will never taste the real joy of life.

So go on, give, never stop giving, no matter how little you have. Of course, you need to have the right intention for giving. For the sake of making someone smile. Give for bringing ease and goodness to the life of someone. Give for the sake of giving.

The most important part of giving is, to give unconditionally without expecting anything in return, not even a thank you. Actually, you will want to give and run away to save the face of those who were given.

On the other hand, the worst kind of giving is the conditional kind. Giving for getting an acknowledgement, giving for fame or praise, this kind of giving will never bring you goodness. It will only feed your ego. So watch out and never fall in this trap.

Your trauma will teach you to give generously, give with love, give with thought and again, give for the sake of giving.

One beautiful act of giving is, giving when you are in need yourself. This kind of giving is the most precious one. It not only brings lots of goodness to you and those who received, but it also turns on a very strong ray of light in your heart that helps you find gains in your losses and find joy in every situation, no matter how dark it can be.

So in times of trauma and loss; the best thing to do is to give, give and give. This will have magic results in your journey. It will also drive you closer and closer to your true being. This is because when you give you are being part of someone else's healing journey and therefore helping them to get close to their true self. Which all means a collective healing and saving is happening, how powerful that can be. This is the beauty of giving, a snowballing of goodness!

Decisions

You will learn to follow your 'gut' feeling. You will learn to follow your heart. You will have an intuition that you can trust and rely on. This is because, this journey allowed you to return to your true soul, it made you reconnect to the source of peace, love and compassion.

You tried what everyone else used to advise you and tried following your mind, but it did not work for you, because you are living your truth now. It will be easy for you to listen to what your heart and soul say to you and decide upon that. This will make you live an authentic life, which was exclusively made for you. Many choose to follow the path of others, ignoring the loud advice of their souls, these will never taste the sweetness of living an authentic, truthful life. You could have been one of them if you did not go through your loss. Be thankful for it!

You now can be the one and only author of your life book. Without any interference from anyone else. You will be free. You will be true. Some people will go, you will not mind as you already tasted 'losing' many. The good ones will always be around, no matter what you decide. They will actually push you to follow your truth.

Yes, sometimes, some decisions will take you to uncertain destinations. But believe me, my friend, these are the ones which are full of wonder. What meaning can life have without venture. Never resist, if you ever find yourself in a vague situation, watch out with excitement, as mystery is the way to mastery.

Keeping busy

One of the best ways to feel that you have a purpose, that you are more than your sorrow, more than your loss and more than your pain is to keep going, no matter what.

Keeping yourself busy does not mean that you distract yourself from fully feeling, expressing and releasing your pain, no, you can still release it fully, slowly and take as much time as you need.

Keeping busy is to keep you going.

Yes, sometimes, some prefer to shut off the world, take time off, but until when and does that mean that what you are going through has put the world on hold? Well, it does not, because life keeps moving, life keeps going; it does not stop for or because of anyone. Indeed, after realising the trauma it is a good idea to keep our focus on the positive things in our lives, on being productive and realising that life keeps going; it did not stop or pause for us to deal with our loss. So we should not miss out on more of what is left of our lives by pausing.

Keeping busy can actually open doors for you; it can actually be part of the healing process. It can inspire you with ways and strategies to get out of your sorrow and to find joy instead.

If we decide to switch off the world, take time off and give up on ourselves altogether, our focus will be on our hardships and negative thoughts which will make us feel even worse and can cause depression and we can lose hope easily.

The more you keep busy, especially with doing good things, helping and serving others, the easier you will get through this time and it will make your healing journey an exciting, productive one.

Plant a tree, learn a new skill, read a book or volunteer, just keep yourself occupied and all this will help you unfold your true self.

Just start

When you have great ideas, you know that you are capable of them, otherwise you would not have been inspired with them. Then you get over-whelmed asking yourself:

How am I going to do it? Where will I find the time? Who do I think I am? And many other un-helpful questions.

The secret, easy answer to all the above is: Just start!

Start, and the doors will start to open for you. Start and the river will flow. Start and things will start to move in the right direction, and you will start to see that you *are* doing it and more im-portantly that you are successful in doing it.

Say no to hesitation.

I remember one day rushing for the bus, for some reason I could see it, but it turned earlier than expected, even if I ran, I would not catch it. I said to myself, why not trying signalling to the driver, I mean it is worth trying, Diline! My naughty self was saying to me: this will never

41

work. I still did it and signalled to the 'kind' driver. The surprise was that he actually stopped a metre before the bus stop, something that drivers never usually do. I was thankful and got on the bus with a big smile.

This all happened in seconds and I had to make the decision in less than that, but it made me think; how many times have I listened to that naughty voice, and how many opportunities have I missed because of this. Since then, I have learned to always try, to give it a go. It does not matter if it does not work, at least you made an effort and tried.

Do not make the assumption that it is not going to work or that it is too late. Opportunities sometimes only come once in life, so go for it, try. Stop hesitation. You never know, you might be sent kind souls, just like our bus driver who will help you to reach your destination without delay.

Imagine always having this attitude, how many opportunities will you catch that you used to think were impossible? Also, imagine having the attitude of that bus driver, how amazing to think of the number of successes you will be part of. Just start, give it a go, and encourage others on your way too.

You will know no worries

Because you will know that what is meant for you will chase you. You will not worry because you will live your moment fully and be aware that you have now, and now is all you have. And because of this, now is what is worth investing your energy and good thoughts on.

The future should not be something that you have any concerns about because it may never come. Now is what is guaranteed, so you learn to enjoy it and think the best will always come because you have, you.

Detach yourself from people and worldly things

One of the lessons that people can fail to learn until they go through a trauma is, detachment. In a world that keeps pushing you to be attached to material and meaningless things, a world that keeps promoting the idea that you need someone or some things to make you happy, your hardship comes to wake you up from all this; to teach you to detach.

You can become detached from everyone and everything around you, no matter how close you are to them, this of course does not take away the sincere love that you have for them, for example your parents or your children.

Detachment is, knowing that you do not own them and they do not own you, as we are all free spirits. Detachment is about unconditional love, allowing yourself and those around you the freedom to be as they are. You feel happy and content with your own company, when you arrive to this point, no one can ever disturb your peace, no matter what they surprise you and do!

When you master detachment, you will experience an infinite happiness.

You will be free

You will stop wasting any effort in resisting events and things. You will not judge. You will not be attached. This is the sum of all freedoms. Freedom is to free you from yourself.

How?

Sometimes you, yes you, can be the one who imprisons yourself in the smallest cage. The prison of your own mind, when you limit it with limiting thoughts, when you limit it with fears, worries and negativities.

When you limit yourself with concerns of what people are going to say or think. When you limit it with making judgements about everyone you meet, instead of focusing on yourself and respecting their journey.

You also imprison yourself with resistance, when you resist things or events that happen to you, instead of allowing the water to flow smoothly. You only bring more of what you resist without you realising. Do not resist, let it be and it will pass.

You imprison yourself when you attach yourself

to material things, places or people. This will tie your happiness to having them in your life, if you lose them, you feel lost.

You will never taste the true freedom until you master acceptance, and a non-judgemental and detached way of life.

Silence

There is something magical about silence that no language in the world can ever express. Falling into silence helps you to better understand what you are going through.

When you are silent, the greatest ideas evolve. When you are silent, you get to meet with yourself. You get to unfold yourself. You get to face your own weaknesses and flaws. You get to know your strengths, dreams and more.

Silence familiarises you with who you are.

When we are too busy in our lives that are full of noise and drama, when things get overwhelming, the best thing to do for yourself is to take it away, far away. Away from the noise, away from the crowds and fall into silence. Yes, sometimes you cannot to do that, but you can train yourself to be in silence even in the noisiest places.

This can be achieved through controlling your mind, switching off all your thoughts and merely taking the time to be. You can do this by focusing on one object and observing it or even observing your hand and how it moves; this can make you appreciate it more. You will realise that sometimes some will be intimidated by your silence, let them be.

One who does not understand your silence, will never be able to understand you if you speak and will always have something to mis-interpret.

The power of words

As your loss teaches you the power of silence, it also teaches you the power of words.

You will know the impact of the words that you whisper to yourself every day. You will learn to say good things about yourself to yourself. You will learn to use good words, which are full of love and kindness to yourself. When you start to do this, it will be easy for you to do the same to people; good words will come out of you naturally without any effort or hesitation. You will encourage people, say kind words and be happy for their joy and success.

You will be appreciative and say thank you always as you will know how important that is.

Words have the power to lift someone up, they can also put many down. You learn to think before you speak, if it is not something nice you will keep it to yourself.

Words can heal. They can create anxiety and fear. Choose to heal. Words can be spoken or written, written can leave a more lasting impact.

I will never forget a few words from my lecturer in the last year of university, he emailed me to say that he was grateful for my contributions in class and that I made him think hard and reflect on his own views. These words might have taken him a few minutes to type, but they left a lasting effect on me – feeling acknowledged and understanding the power of my own words, how they influenced a respected expert in Counselling Psychology; it all gave me more courage and confidence in myself. Here I am mentioning this, to show my appreciation for his words. I feel this played a role in my journey towards knowing the power of words, and deciding to share mine with the world in this book.

This is a message to you all, to stress the importance of saying the good that you see in people; do not keep it to yourselves. Do not assume that they understand that you think this about them; no, they cannot read your mind. So please, if you have something nice to say to anyone about themselves, do it now, be part of their self-discovery. Be part of uplifting their spirits and building a beautiful memory in their mind and be a lasting part of their journey.

How many good words about someone have you kept stuck in your mouth or heart without saying them, how many times have you seen a good thing in someone without acknowledging it? And why was this the case? Were you too proud to say it? Were you too jealous? Too envious? Could saying these words have scratched your ego?

The good thing about your trauma is it cleanses you from all these diseases of the heart that disturb the peace. It purifies your heart from hate as you will accept everyone as they are; your heart will be pure of envy and jealousy as you will enjoy seeing good happen to other people.

This makes it very easy for you to be a source of goodness in this world, to everyone through your words and more. Let your words bring life back to tired souls.

I love how the Qur'an describes a good word as a good, proud tree with strong roots, which keeps giving fruits abundantly. This is truly how good words have a lasting effect on the heart, just like the words of the lecturer.

Purification

Going through loss can be a process of purifying of yourself if you choose to follow this path. It involves physical, mental and spiritual purification.

It will take time. The more time you keep hold of your pain and the negative emotions, the more time you will need to purify yourself, but it is never too late. You will notice the magical results of this process. Any negative results that your body suffered, will slowly fade away, this happens because your soul is more connected with your body and you are enlightened with who you really are.

Deeper and more complicated medical conditions which might have accrued due to your trauma, will also start to heal if you consciously and intentionally work on this. If you acknowledge that these conditions happened because you were not connected with yourself, because you were not looking after yourself and you never acknowledged or dealt with your trauma and the overwhelming emotions. Now you know, and you are dealing with it. You are starting the process of healing and curing yourself. It will take time. But with consistent and continuous intentional work and much self-love, it will work.

Go on, start the process from today.

You need to talk to yourself and re-programme your thoughts. This can be through a 'love letter' to yourself. It can be by going somewhere special with the intention of making it the beginning of your healing and purifying journey.

This will be the lasting cure for all your illnesses. Even medicine will be more effective if you do have to take any. Through going back to your true self, you can release all those negative emotions, all those sorrows, worries and mistakes. Set them free to free you. You will be a healthy being, inside and out!

The purification is not only going to happen to your body, but more importantly it will happen to your mind, heart and soul, and cure those diseases of the heart that many human beings struggle with – whether this was jealousy, envy, hatred, love of power or greed or more.

Purification needs to be closely monitored. The heart is the heart of everything, so if you keep on track with the state of your heart, this small magical pump, if you keep it pure, your life will be pure of any pain. It will be pure from any trouble. A troubled heart will find a problem in every situation. It will see everything and everyone through the eye of criticism. A pure heart sees everything and everyone through the eye of appreciation. A brave heart chooses love.

The trauma of loss can be a path to purifying yourself from the diseases of the heart which cause disturbance to your inner peace and the peace of the world around you. The trauma is a way to wake you up, to show you how many worldly things are insignificant; it will teach you empathy and sympathy and to never compare yourself to anyone else.

This loss happened for you to gain your pure child-like heart back. Celebrate your purity, embrace it, and keep a close eye on it!

You realise your true age

We get asked sometimes: how old are you? Can our life be counted merely by numbers? I do not think so. Through your trauma you will learn this lesson:

Our life and age are counted by moments and by the feelings we had in those moments. How many years have we aged in moments of betrayal, moments of pain or lack of support? And how many years younger have we become in a moment of appreciation or a moment of joy?

When we felt so loved, unconditionally loved, only because we are who we are. Those are the moments that define our lives, the moments that make life worth living.

Your age is not the number of years you lived. It is the number of moments that you experienced living. You can be 70 but have a young 20-year-old soul due to having many joyful moments in your life. And you can be 20 but have aged many years older due to experiencing many betrayals, pain and misery in your life without dealing with them.

Make your life count. Make your trauma an opportunity to grow but not to age.

Have control of your emotions and always feel the joy whatever you are going through. You can always find the light in every situation if you decide to.

Home will also have a different meaning

Home is where you feel safe, welcome, loved and most importantly: appreciated, when you know, accept and love yourself. Your loss will teach you that any place you go to can become home. You will learn that the space and place do not matter; what matters is who you take there, with all the complexities of the internal world inside of you.

If your internal self is happy and content; you will bring happiness and contentment anywhere you go, no matter what features the place has or what part of the world it is, you will feel Home. If your internal world is troubled, you will bring trouble and disturb anywhere you go, and nowhere on the whole planet will ever feel Home to you.

You make Home, with the smells, tastes, feelings, sounds and the atmosphere, all can come from you wherever you are.

Because now, you will understand that: You are Home.

Things to help you in the healing journey

Walking

Walking has magic effects. It helps you regain your focus. It helps you clear your mind and get clarity about where you are. When you get 'triggered', walk. It will help you gain control of your emotional response. When you have an overwhelming day, walk. It will help you relax. When you are not able to make a decision about anything small or big, walk. You will be inspired about the right decision after that.

If life throws betrayals or events that can break your heart, walk. It will help you process it with calmness; it will help you wash any negative feelings towards anyone and become more at peace with yourself and them.

Shake off all the sorrows, anger and flames that are inside of you. The more you walk, the more you will shake. Walking is an example, but any physical activity helps too.

You are carrying a burden of negative thoughts, emotions and energies that you kept within you without dealing with them. Your physical and spiritual being are carrying this and you need to move and move to shake it all off your shoulders. This can be walking, running, swimming or something else – any physical activity, the more of it, the better.

This proved very effective with the wonderful refugee children who I work with. The beautiful thing is that they managed to express their need for this by asking for more physical activities. We started organising more of these activities, which resulted in increasing their emotional wellbeing and they showed less post traumatic disorder symptoms.

Talking

Talking to someone who you really trust makes a huge difference. It helps you share the pain with someone who can understand. Even if they cannot do anything to help you, knowing that someone is there with an open heart and actually listening to what you have to say, helps you un-tie the knots that you have in your mind; it helps you to have clarity about your own situation.

On the other hand, when you keep things to yourself for so long some thoughts that you never needed can grow and become bigger and bigger, then stick in your mind and become 'beliefs' that stop you from fulfilling your potential. Keeping hold of negative thoughts can also create a negative thought snowball, which can all cause anxiety, disorders and depression.

So please, let it out, talk it out.

You are most blessed if you have someone you trust, who can actively listen to you and helps you see sense and minimise the size of the issue that you have.

Good friendships

A good, kind and truthful friend can be enough for you. Someone who you can trust. Someone who you can count on to listen to all you need to dump out of you, to be able to move on. All you need is a friend who listens and tells you with a reassuring voice: 'something good will come out of this' or that 'you are doing great.'

This or any other reassuring words can work like a sea breeze on your burning heart. These words will cool it all down and bring you back on track. A good friend can also make you see humour in what you are going through, who makes you laugh when you want to shout out crying. Someone who 'contains' you. If you find this person, you are one lucky soul. You can only find them if you, yourself are one of them!

Writing

If you do not feel comfortable talking or if you struggle to find the right person to talk to, then writing is the right option for you; get a pen and paper and write. Write all the 'garbage' out of you, you can read it or rip it up after; this will be up to you. The most important thing is it will all be out of your system now. Your body and soul are set free from all the adverse effects that holding negative thoughts can cause.

Art

Art is a great way to express yourself. Expressing yourself is extremely important.

I know sometimes we are driven away from expressing ourselves, because of fear of judgement or being misunderstood, so we choose to keep things to 'rot' in us. But this is not what you are here for, you are here to express everything within you and share it with the world. You have your very own unique knowledge, wisdom and creativity that no one else has. When you decide to box this all in and fail to express it, you stop some of your goodness coming out, goodness which can benefit many of your fellow humans.

Do not choose this path. Choose to share. Choose to care and most importantly, choose to leave a legacy for the world that many will benefit from, even after you leave.

Whatever you leave un-expressed will leave a scar within you and one scar after another will turn into an illness, whether it is physical or mental. So guard yourself, avoid all this and express yourself, go on! No need to shy away. Any artwork will be a great way to do that.

Let your pain out through art. The focus you give to art, charges you with a great amount of positive energy. The ideas will flow one after another. Go on, try some art, and create many beautiful things. When you choose to do this, all your pain will be in vain.

Painting is one art form that gets everything within you, out of you. It is a great way to empty yourself from yourself; from all the negative thoughts, memories and experiences.

Yes, I know, you are going to say: 'I cannot paint' or 'I have no artistic skills.' The good news is that you do not need to have any artistic skills, and I can assure you that you and everyone else can paint! All you need is some paper, or any object you prefer, and paint, any kind will do. Mixing the paint is the most fun part; mix all the colours, any colour you fancy with the other. Sometimes your mood can affect your choice of colour, but that does not matter, just mix and paint anyway, anywhere and anytime you feel you need to get this negative energy out, these disturbing thoughts or any burden off your chest, paint.

You will be surprised how much better you will feel every time you do this. Go on, try it and you will never regret it.

Fasting

Fasting is the chosen hunger that teaches you to be humble. You starve with joy, well that is at the start. Then you will not notice the need for that feeding habit of yours. Fasting will minimise the significance of your loss in your eyes. It will strengthen the connection with your soul that you lost over time. It will boost your patience; it will give you power.

Fasting gives you clarity and fuels you with energy. It will teach gratitude and generosity. Fasting will make you understand that the real food is the one that you feed your soul with, not your body. Through fasting, you will win over your desires and that will be the real victory!

Breathe

You might be saying that everyone breathes any-way and every day, but do they really?

Breathe deeply, intentionally and with your full soul. Deep and deeply, through your nose, breath-ing out all the 'junk' within you through your mouth, wait; this has to be very slowly. Breathe deeply in and very slowly out.

Do this every day, morning and night even if just seven times each time and trust me you will see a big difference in how you feel, in your physical body and your mood.

This is the smallest but most significant thing that you can do to yourself, to your soul and to your body. It is your right to breathe, breathe and breathe.

So please, go on, breathe, deeply in and very, very slowly out.

Heal through nature

Connecting with nature is a great way of healing from difficulties and loss; this can be through contemplating and connecting with natural habitats and fully using your senses while you're in nature.

Contemplate

Contemplation is the key to the right path. It is a neglected act that human beings turned away from, as they do not see it as a priority in the midst of their busy schedules. All the mountains, rivers, waterfalls, birds and more are things that you pass by without noticing or giving them their right of appreciation. Magnificent natural events take place around us, which we turn a blind eye towards.

Sunrise is a great example of this. It takes place every single day but hardly anyone makes any effort to witness it. To enjoy the big event of the re-birth of a new day, this brings the message of the re-birth of you. To witness the rays of light coming slowly, slowly out from the horizon, what a sacred thing to be honoured to watch and con-template.

You can attend this event every day for free if you make the effort and find the right spot and wake up early, of course! It might be free, but it has an endless amount of energy that you can charge yourself with whenever you watch it. It reminds you of the gift of life that you are being given every day, a new day, when many were not given this opportunity. It also reminds you that miracles happen all around you.

It encourages you to do more and to be more. It pushes you towards the right path for you. Then another great event ends the day: sunset. It comes to open the door of reflection.

Have you given this day its right? Were you grateful enough for the new opportunity that you were given? Have you made someone's day, or helped someone? Have you considered the feelings of your fellow humans, stopped yourself saying or doing something that can hurt someone? Have you watered a plant or fed a bird? Have you been kind to yourself?

Or

Have you wasted the day moaning, complaining or blaming?

Well, it is all your choice at the end of the day, how you treat the blessing of a new day with a magical sunrise.

Yes, you have been through a lot, you have lost much but you are still here. You have, you and there is a good reason for that. You are still here for a good cause that you have all the capacity to fulfil if you choose to.

Sunrise teaches us to be grateful all the time in all circumstances and places. You will learn to always be grateful and therefore you will always be given more things to be grateful for.

Trees

Choose to be like them. They adapt to different seasons. They face countless storms. Nonetheless they are always giving.

Their shade is a place of tranquillity.

Their fruits are the source of satisfaction.

Their being is a source of beauty.

The more you connect with trees through the journey, the easier it will be.

Waterfalls

They have special joy around them. Starting with the beauty of water falling from high up to low down, to lift your spirits from down to up. Waterfalls teach you giving and adventure. They teach unity and wonder. They are very powerful; they can fuel you with the strength you need for a while.

Waterfalls are made to remind you that falls are not necessarily always negative. Falls are not here to break you or cause you pain. They prove that some falls are just like these drops of water, which fall to rejoin the stream and follow the right flow.

The sound, oh how it refreshes your mind and waters your heart generously with pure fresh thoughts. The smell around waterfalls clears your lungs and nose from all the dust of the city. Waterfalls are a great example that falls are for you to submit to the forces of nature, to follow the gravity, to go back to your true you.

Go to a waterfall and learn to follow the stream without any resistance. When you do this, you will become your strongest and most generous self, just like a waterfall.

Mountains

When you see them, you remember how small you are. You remember how small the space you are inhabiting in the universe is, compared to those magnificent creatures. Do not fall into the trap of judging from the appearance though. Despite of their significant size, you are much more significant than they are. Those mountains were not given the power of thinking and logic as you were. You are a chosen one. You have those powers. You have the power to climb those mountains if you wished.

They do not have the power of figuring out how you managed to do that. You were trusted to maintain these mountains and the place they settle in, the Earth. You are not here to waste your journey regretting your losses or past. Those happened to remind you of your role and significance on this Earth, that the overwhelming attachment to whatever was 'lost' distracted you from achieving.

Seeds

Seeds, those tiny beings, are great teachers. They remind you that one day, you were one of them and look how far you have come. Interacting with the soil brings you back to your true self; it reconnects you with your nature. Sowing a small seed, watching it grow slowly, fuels you with patience and hope. It gives you something to look forward to. As you look after, nourish and water, as you care for these little seeds, your true soul is nourished and will flourish too.

A seed also teaches you that no matter how insignificant you now feel or how dark it can seem as a result of your loss, a big tree, with some abundant harvest will come out of you, if you choose the path which the seed has chosen; the path of growth.

Listen

The sound of birds will become your best melody. You will notice the beautiful singing of the little robin that came especially for you to deliver messages full of hope. Listen to the sound of rain and remember; as this water is driven to the needy ground to flourish, good things will be driven your way too.

That pigeon that you used to complain about, came to whisper in your ear that you can do anything you wish for if you listen to your heart. Only when you can master the language of your heart you can understand all the unspoken languages of the world.

Try it; listen.

Touch

Touch that soil that you started from

Touch it when you are in pain and the pain will be in vain

Touch it when you are anxious and you feel at peace

Touch it when you are disconnected and you will be back on track

Touch it when you are all over the place and it will put you back together

Touch the grass, touch the trees

Touch the river and dip into the stream

Touch the sand of the beach and swim into the sea

Touch to be back in touch with who you really are

Smell

When that breeze brought you that fresh smell of elderflower, it was not a coincidence. It came especially for you to spring joy into your heart. Smell. It has the ability to take you back to a meaningful memory you had in a special place. It can also take you to places that you have never visited. Places that feel like heaven. Oh, that lavender, how it brings calm and rest to your mind.

That pure jasmine can take you beyond the oceans to that little corner where you sneaked those little flowers to make that necklace. Or that smell of grass that refreshes your place on a sunny day.

The joy of the smell of a needy ground when it is blessed with water on a rainy day.

That smell of pine was made to get you back on the line.

And the beauty of the scent of cypress, was made specially to lift you when you feel helpless.

Smell the smell of the beach to become out of reach.

These smells and more.

Were made for you to explore.

Start to enjoy them more than before.

Breathe them deeply in and get all the trauma and stress out of your body.

Replace them with those smells of joy, peace and calmness.

Look and see

Look through the eye of a child so you can see the beauty of the universe. Look through the eye of a child so you can see goodness in every person.

It is ironic how the more 'adult' we become, the less able we are to express our needs and the things which can help us heal, progress and improve in life. Interacting with children makes you more grounded and more connected with your inner child. Look to see and free yourself from every privilege when you see.

See through your eyes and notice the beauty around you. Yes, looking is the job of the eye but the clearest vision comes through your hearts. Open eyes can never truly see through a blind heart. Blind eyes can always fully and clearly see through an open heart.

An innocent smile

On the way home after a long day, sitting on the bus trying to figure out if I had a productive day

An innocent smile catches my eye

Made me forget the busyness of the day

I smile back, then she acts shy

Then smiles with joy in her eye

Children, interacting with them is good for the soul

They see you as you are

They are free from any privilege, ill thoughts, doubts that adulthood can build and stop one from seeing the beauty in the other

Go back to your true you, to that child within you who sees goodness in everyone

Learn how to smile, laugh and be happy without expectations

Be the happiness, be the joy and be the light that everyone needs

Pray

I kept the best for last as they say!

The most beautiful, satisfying and miraculous way to heal of all is, to pray. Well, you can actually do it as part of contemplation, but when you do it separately with all the focus of your soul and spirit, miracles take place. When you liberate yourself from yourself, from your ego, from all the reliance you had on anyone but God, when you come submissive and 'naked' from all the material things in life–this submissiveness is the true liberation of the self.

You will only taste the real freedom, the most precious value that human beings have been striving for throughout history, when you fully submit to Him.

Pray and speak all you have in your heart. Without any barriers, shame, boundaries or prestige; let it all out. You do not need a priest, a sheikh, a monk or any mediator to come between you and God.

Ask Him to purify you, as when you are pure and have a pure heart, everything else will come to you even without you asking for it.

The outcome

Celebrating the re-birth of your authentic self

A new you. You will notice it in every detail of your life. You will notice it in your face. You will feel it in your heart. You will see it in your interactions with people and other creatures around you. Everything about you will be nice, new and fresh. A new better version of you.

Well, this is the person that you are meant to be. The person that you were born to become. Your mother did not go through that long exhausting labour for you to suffer. She did not go through that for you to be a victim. Her pain was for you to fulfil your highest potential.

Never think of yourself as a 'loser' or a 'victim'. This journey will be worth it, when you choose to be worthy. When you choose to be the powerful one, even in your weakest moments. This will always lead you to winning, success and endless abundance.

Your face will change – a lot

Oh yes! You will look at pictures of yourself and compare them to old ones, then ask yourself: is this me! As you are more truthful to your soul and live on that path; change not only happens inside you but also on the outside. You can clearly notice that on your face. Your skin returns to your first skin, like a baby, nice and soft. You will always see light in it and your eyes will always be shining with purity.

This will make anyone who sees you happy. You will not take it personally. You will know that it is the light of your soul they are seeking. Because they see the source that made them in you, and human beings always yearn for where they belong: their divine belonging. Even if they resist acknowledging it.

You will be content

You will always see positivity and goodness in everyone and every situation whether it was a betrayal, loss or whenever things go 'wrong'. This is because you have peace within you. You are at peace with who you are.

No one on Earth can ever 'trigger' you, you will no longer experience such thing and this word will no longer exist in your dictionary. Because you are in control of your thoughts, emotions and actions. Inner peace is the key to outer peace.

There is trouble in our world today because many struggle to gain inner peace. The more we have people who are at peace with themselves, the more peace we will witness in the world.

As you are always at peace and content in the face of whatever life throws at you, you will spread peace too. This can be through a smile that does not leave your face. You will be happy to spread some light and inspire thirsty souls who are still in the beginning of their journey.

Your trauma favoured you. It allowed you to

progress years ahead of many of your fellow humans. You will feel privileged to support them to get to where you did. You will see all the wisdom behind what you went through. You will see the wisdom in what you thought was a 'loss' at the time.

You will have witnessed each and every step of the extraordinary plan which was made especially for you. You will be very grateful for it all. You will be grateful for everything and everyone who has been part of your journey, including the ones who caused you harm. You will appreciate your life much more than before, as every morning will be an occasion to celebrate a new opportunity

Every fall will be appreciated for the lessons which were learned from it.

You will be grateful for having dreams for your life, for being able to wish for and imagine them, which will make them run towards you and become real.

Love is the secret of life

You will see love in everything because you will finally understand that you are the love. You will stop wasting your time looking in the wrong places, because all the love is in you and from you.

You will watch people being jealous, envious, greedy or dealing with other diseases of the heart and will smile and wish them peace and purification. You will pray that they taste the joy of love, which you got to enjoy because of what you thought was a loss.

Your loss was for you to experience this infinite love and joy by finding yourself. If you find yourself, you never really lost anything. Finding yourself is the key to finding everything else missing in or from your life.

You will inspire many to experience love. You are full of love because your source is never ending. Your source is heavenly. Your source is divine. You will inspire others to find their way to the divine love too. Love will be your lasting legacy.

Love

Love is to see everything through the eye of beauty

Love cannot see faults and that is the beauty of love

When you have love, you do not expect anything from anyone

When you have love, you do not analyse too much or judge

You do not blame or criticise

Love brings you joy and happiness

Love gives you courage and truthfulness

It can treat all illnesses

Love gives you hope

It fuels you with patience

Love gives you wisdom and power

It revives you from all ill thoughts and diseases of the heart

It takes you back to your nature

Love pushes you to be your true self, without being em-

barrassed or apologetic

Love will guide you through and help you grow

Love is the secret of life; the real true life

As there are many people alive but have no life

The more connected to your soul you are, the more love you will have. Through love all the other good things evolve.

When you are full of love, things like giving, forgiving, letting go and making peace will happen by default without any effort.

Love starts from within, you need to love yourself first, and you need to love your soul, care for it and give it. Love yourself with all your flaws, faults and weaknesses. Love all the unique and beautiful about you

When you do this, you will be able to give love in the most beautiful way. When you do this, everything and everyone will love you in a sincere way.

And if you are looking for love, do not look in the wrong places. It is all in you and from you.

I end this book with this love note, and whisper to you that...

You will change, yes, but this is the human being that you were always meant to be, that you kept ignoring and hesitating to be. You kept trying to drive yourself away from you. Until now finally you listened to your soul and re-tuned to your true authentic self who will serve the role that was created for this world, that no one except you can fulfil in the most creative, enjoyable and efficient way.

Yes, you my dear friend needed to go through this loss, to shake you, to wake you and to make you, YOU.

You needed to go through the pain of loss, to experience the joy of finding your truth. To reconnect you with your beautiful being, soul and spirit.

Go on, celebrate the Re-birth of yourself, the day that your body, soul and spirit are all connected and start to flourish, the day that you find yourself is the actual day that you were born – your real birthday.

Acknowledgements

I would like to sincerely thank the wonderful 'sister in the journey' as she loves to be called Na'ima B Robert, the best coach I could ask for. Her validity to my message, encouragement and golden calls, made this book come to light.

I would also love to thank Hend Hegazi, for her consistent support, soft messages through the writing, editing, re-editing and publishing journey. Without her commitment and patience with me this also wouldn't have been possible.

Big thanks to the line editor, my genuine friend and sister: Catherine Ouhib.

Thank you to my writing fellow Tumkeen, who volunteered to design the first draft of the cover and amazingly managed to do it 'so me' without needing to know much about me!

Also, thanks to Susie Poole for playing a key role in putting this book together and making it look cool.

Thank you to all the wonderful members of my 'book squad'. I appreciate each and every one of you for being the first readers of my book.

A very special, warm and love-filled THANK YOU to my beloved Zainedine. Your poster did the trick, habeeby!

Lastly and most importantly, I thank my lord, who has put the message of the book in my heart and sent all the above to my path to help me share it with the world. Alhamdo le Allah.

About the Author

Diline is a Palestinian British author living in Scotland. After graduating from university, she started supporting refugee families and young people to overcome their traumas. She also works on supporting different causes including social justice and climate change.

Diline found writing a great way to fulfil her passion of inspiring and helping others to heal themselves and live a grounded life.

In her free time, you will find Diline in the zone, painting or crafting or maybe walking amongst the trees. But if it's dinner time, she will turn to a chef; throwing the many herbs that she enjoyed growing!